September 12th

We Knew Everything Would Be All Right

Written and illustrated by first-grade students
of H. Byron Masterson Elementary
in Kennett, Missouri

SCHOLASTIC INC.

New York   Toronto   London   Auckland   Sydney
Mexico City   New Delhi   Hong Kong

Dedicated to all of our families

We like to feel secure and safe.
Somedays, the rut is the best place to be.

Copyright © 2002 by Scholastic Inc
Scholastic and associated logos are trademarks and/or registered trademarks of Scholastic Inc
ISBN 0-439-44246-X

12 11 10 9 8 7 6 5 4

Book Design by Bill Henderson
Printed and bound in the U.S.A.

First Printing, July 2002

Meet the Authors

KENNETT SCHOOL DISTRICT

First Grade Class, H. Byron Masterson Elementary School, Kennett, MO

Standing, left to right: Rebecca Smith, Jay Edgington, Kayla McBay, Jamie Ellington, Cameron Harper, William Thomas, Anna Kay Hilburn, Amy Johnson, Keisha Walker, Brian Stracener

Sitting, left to right: Chandler Agee, Jordan Garza, Josh Harmon, Jordan Tefft, Bryce McPherson, Monique Gray, Onterria Carter, Shawn Birmingham

On September 11, 2001, many bad things happened.

September 12th
was a new day.
We knew
everything
would be all
right.

because...

Sunday	Monday	Tuesday	Wednesday	Thursday	Friday	Saturday
						1
2	3	4	5	6	7	8
9	10	11	12			

September 2001

the sun came up and

the birds started
to sing again.

We came to school the same way.

We knew everything would be all right when we saw our teacher smiling at the door.

We said the pledge like always.

We sang the National Anthem very loudly.

Aa Bb Cc Dd Ee Ff Gg Hh Ii Jj Kk Ll Mm Oo Pp Qq Rr Ss Tt Uu Vv Ww Xx Yy Zz

Our teacher sat and read us lots of good books.

Mrs. Robertson

We had recess again.

We knew everything would be all right
because we had homework.

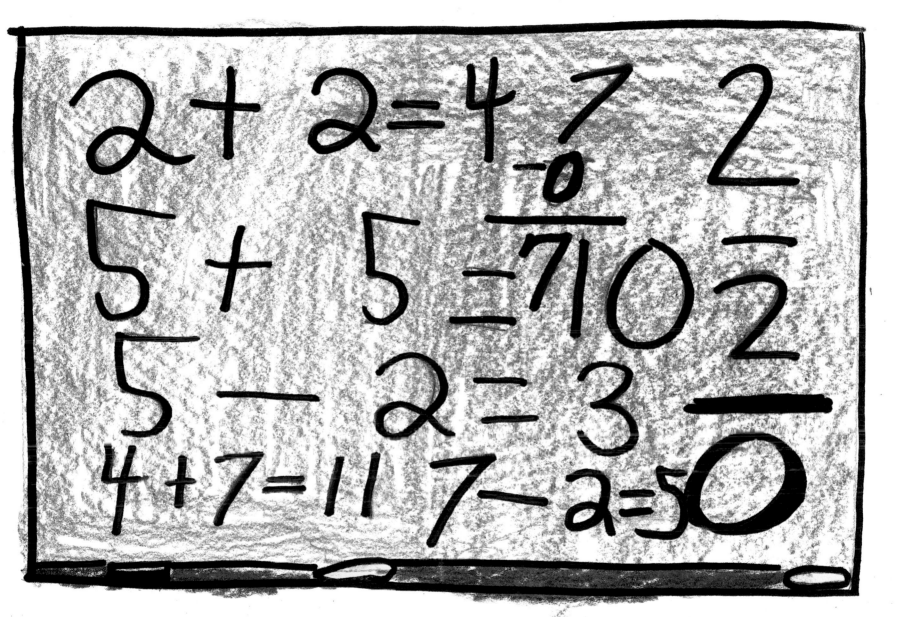

2+2 still added up to 4.

Our thought for the day became "America United."

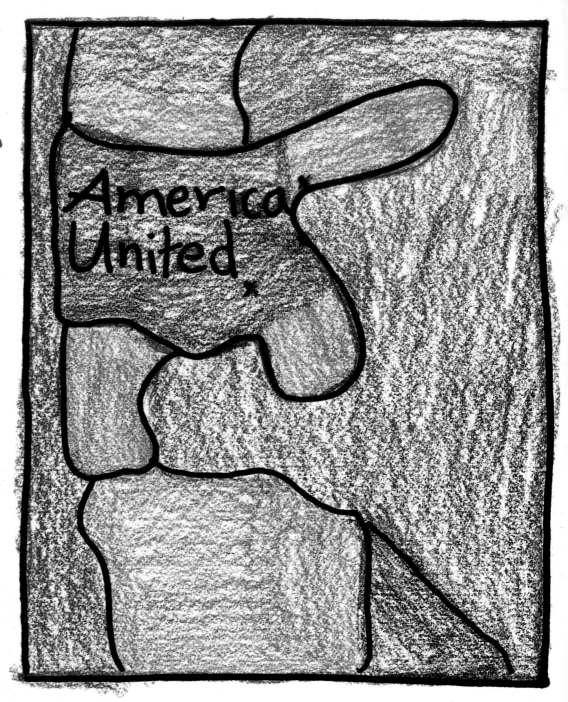

We saw
lots of flags.

Red, white and blue suddenly became
everyone's favorite colors.

On television we heard our President tell us everything would be all right.

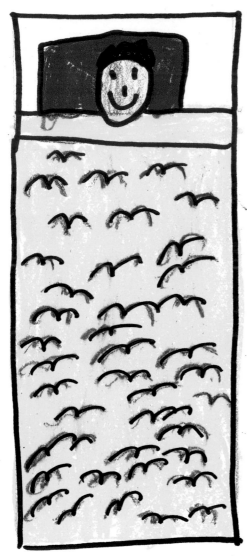

On September 12th, our parents
still tucked us in our warm, safe beds.

Our parents talked to us about the bad things that had happened the day before.

We knew we would be all right
because our parents said they loved us.

We knew everything would be all right because the stars and moon came out and America went to sleep.

And the next morning
the sun came up again.